WORDPOWER 3

Helen H. McLullich

Illustrated by
Ray Mutimer and Jon Davis

Oliver & Boyd

Contents

UNIT 1

Boots, Beads and Bloomers

(a)

(b)

(c)

(d)

(e)

 A. Group discussion

1 Would all the clothes shown on pages 4 and 5 be suitable today? Give reasons.

2 Who sets the fashions? Why do they change?

3 Which clothes do you like wearing? Why do you?

> **Spelling note!** Can you spell **clothes** correctly?
>
> Look at the word and say it.
> Cover it, write it and check it.
> Were you correct?

4

(f)

(g)

(h)

B. Sentences

Remember – start each sentence with a capital letter and finish with a full stop.

Write sentences about each picture. Make sure you describe the clothing, headgear, footwear and hairstyle so that the reader gets a clear picture in his mind. If you list items, remember this rule about the comma.

> In a sentence, each item in a list is separated by a comma – except the last two items, if they are joined by and.

C. Nouns

Write these four headings in your workbook and under each heading write five **nouns** that are items of clothing or footwear.

Winter Clothing	Sportswear	Uniforms	Protective Clothing

(i)

(j)

(k)

5

D. Competition

Study this competition form and then go on to **E** on page 7.

COMPETITION
Win an Adventure Holiday for Two

What you have to do:

1 Write what the jumbled words are. Each one is an item of clothing.

knaroa	reblza	rempuj	osthrs
thrsi	landass	wumistsi	nillstowegn

2 Write two or three sentences to tell why you would like to win this holiday.

Fill in the coupon, cut it out and send it in an envelope along with your answers to:

HI-FASHION,
12 Petticoat Lane,
Hatrick,
HK39 7AT.

Surname (capitals please) _____

Forename(s) _____

Address _____

_____

_____

Postcode _____

The judge's decision is final.

Closing date – 31st March.

E. Scanning

Scan the advertisement quickly to find the answers.
Make your answers short.

1 Who is offering the prize in the competition?
2 What is the prize?
3 Which part of your name has to be written in capital letters?
4 Write the sentence that tells you it's no use complaining
   if you don't win.
5 What is the last date on which your entry will be accepted?
6 Copy the coupon into your workbook and fill it in.
7 Write the answers to the jumbled words.

F. Writing

FREE
Choose a complete outfit of clothing

Make a sketch of the outfit you would choose. Use the sketch to help you write a description of the clothes. Read your own work and make any corrections you think would improve it.

G. Spelling to, too, two

1 Study the use of **to**, **too** and **two**
  in the pictures.

2 Write these sentences.
  Put **to**, **too** or **two** correctly in the spaces.

  (a) My team scored _____ goals.
  (b) The coffee was _____ hot.
  (c) Their _____ friends went _____ .

3 Make up three sentences to show the use
  of **to**, **too** and **two**.

too tall
TO THE ZOO
two gnus
The dog came too.

7

H. Revision

1 Write (a) the title and (b) the author of this book.

Index

2 (a) What is an index?
  (b) Where is it placed in a book?
  (c) What is its purpose?
  (d) How are the items arranged?

Contents

3 (a) What is a Contents list?
  (b) Where is it placed in a book?
  (c) What is its purpose?
  (d) How are the items arranged?

I. Find out.

The words in the box are items of clothing. Look them up in an encyclopaedia, general knowledge book or a book specially about clothing.

Make a drawing of each one and beside it write, **in your own words**, a short paragraph giving information about it.

crinoline
moccasins
sari
mantilla
kilt
jodhpurs

J. Extra

Collect family photographs that show how fashions change. Find out who the people are and when the photographs were taken.

Make a wall frieze of the photos and write a short paragraph describing each one.

Discuss the finished frieze with your class or group.

Take good care of the photos and make sure they are returned to their owners.

When I looked up, the trees had closed in above my head like a prison roof and I couldn't see the smallest patch of sky or a single star. I couldn't see anything at all. The darkness was so solid around me I could almost touch it.

"Dad!" I called out. "Dad, are you there?"

My small high voice echoed through the forest and faded away. I listened for an answer, but none came.

I cannot possibly describe to you what it felt like to be standing alone in the pitchy blackness of that silent wood in the small hours of the night. The sense of loneliness was overwhelming, the silence was as deep as death, and the only sounds were the ones I made myself. I tried to keep absolutely still for as long as possible to see if I could hear anything at all. I listened and listened. I held my breath and listened again. I had a queer feeling that the whole wood was listening with me, the trees and the bushes, the little animals hiding in the undergrowth and the birds nesting in the branches. All were listening. Even the silence was listening. Silence was listening to silence.

I switched on the torch. A brilliant beam of light reached out ahead of me like a long white arm. That was better. Now at any rate I could see where I was going.

The keepers would also see. But I didn't care about the keepers any more. The only person I cared about was my father. I wanted him back.

I kept the torch on and went deeper into the wood.

"Dad!" I shouted. "Dad! It's Danny! Are you there?"

From *Danny, The Champion of the World* by Roald Dahl

A. Group discussion

1 Can you think of times when silence is frightening?
2 Do you remember a time when you enjoyed being alone?
3 Can you be lonely in a crowd?

✎ B. About the story

First, read the following questions.
Next read the story again.   Keep checking the story
until you can answer all the questions.
Finally answer the questions without turning back to
page 9.

  (a) What is the name of the boy in the story?
  (b) Which words tell that he was quite a young boy?
  (c) Where was he?
  (d) Why was he there?
  (e) Why didn't he switch on his torch sooner?
  (f) What time do you think it was?
  (g) Would you go alone into a dark wood?   Say why
       you would or would not.
  (h) From information given in the story, several things
       might happen next.   Choose two of them and
       write a short paragraph about each.

C. Listening

Are you a good listener?
To help you to find out, your teacher will read to you
part of a story called *The House of Sixty Fathers* by
Meindert DeJong.   It is on page 94 but **only your
teacher** should turn to that page.

  Follow the pictures as the story is being read, then
answer the questions on page 11.

How well did you listen?
Answer in sentences.

1 Why was Tien Pao hiding in a cave?
2 What did Tien Pao do so that no one would hear him crying?
3 What did Tien Pao see when he peered out of the cave?
4 How did Tien Pao feel when he first heard a sound coming
   to him through the darkness?
5 What did he think it was?
6 What did he discover it was?
7 Do you think Tien Pao would be glad to have his pig with him?
   Give reasons.
8 Which do you think Tien Pao would find more
   frightening – the silence or the slight sound?   Give reasons.

D. Similes

Read these sentences.

(a) The trees had closed in above my head **like a
   prison roof**.
(b) The silence was **as deep as death**.
(c) The brilliant beam of light reached out **like a long
   white arm**.

In each sentence one thing is said to be like something
else. This is called using a **simile** Similes make
reading and writing interesting – but don't use them
too often.
   Roald Dahl makes very interesting similes.
Complete the similes below, making yours
interesting too.   Two of them have been done for you.

1 as sharp as a surgeon's scalpel
2 as uncomfortable as _____
3 as thick as _____
4 as spine-chilling as _____

5 to flop like a rag doll
6 to barge in like _____
7 to run like _____
8 to grasp like _____

11

E. Joining words

> 1 My voice echoed through the forest **and** faded away.
> 2 I listened for an answer **but** heard nothing.

Joining words are **conjunctions**.
The conjunctions **and** and **but** are used in the middle of the sentences in the box.   They join two ideas.
The words in the circle are also conjunctions and they may be used at the beginning or in the middle of sentences.

Write these sentences, putting the most suitable conjunction from the circle in each space.
Use each conjunction only once.

if
unless
when
because
although
until

1 Danny was afraid _____ it was so quiet.
2 _____ Tien Pao awoke, it was dark.
3 The keepers would question him _____ they found him.
4 Danny would search _____ he found his Dad.
5 _____ he knew the keepers might see him, he shone his torch.
6 _____ Tien Pao found somewhere to hide, he would be discovered.

  # F. Write a poem.

Read this poem on loneliness.

> Loneliness
>
> Loneliness is being lost in a crowd.
> Loneliness is having no-one to listen to you,
>   No-one to talk to you,
>   To laugh or joke or share thoughts with you
>   Or swap ideas.
> So if you sit all alone it will come.
> You are so very lonely; there is no-one.
>
> Loneliness is having no-one to love you,
> No-one to make sure you have breakfast
>   Before you go out,
>   Having no-one to check your homework,
>   To see it's all right.
> And you think to yourself,
> 'So this is loneliness.'
>   (Janie Struthers, age 10)

What are **your** thoughts on loneliness? Express them in a poem, which need not have rhyming lines.

Conifers to Comics

  Here is a flow chart that shows the stages of paper-making. Study it and describe the stages.

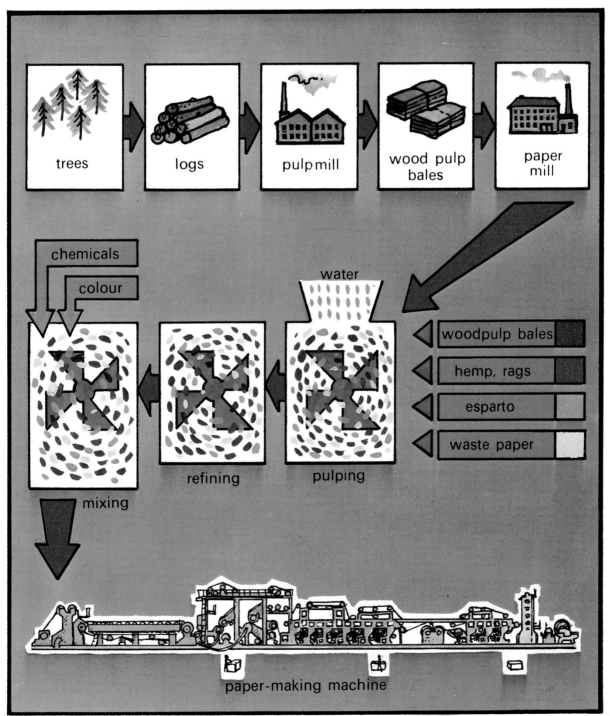

trees → logs → pulp mill → wood pulp bales → paper mill

chemicals
colour

water

woodpulp bales
hemp, rags
esparto
waste paper

mixing ← refining ← pulping

paper-making machine

 ## A. Flow chart

Here is a flow chart to show how toast is made.

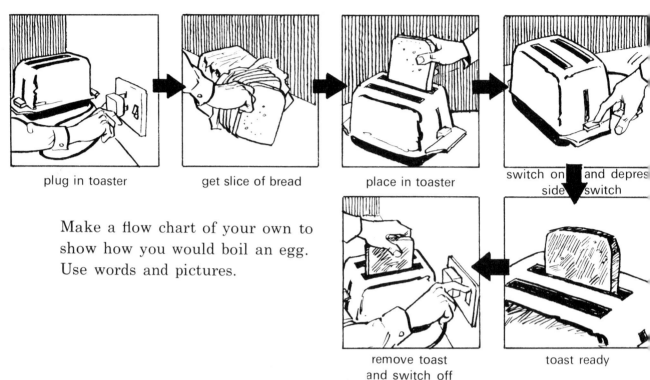

plug in toaster   get slice of bread   place in toaster   switch on and depress side switch

remove toast and switch off   toast ready

Make a flow chart of your own to show how you would boil an egg. Use words and pictures.

B. Uses of paper

Paper has been used for all the things pictured. Make four headings in your workbook.

Home	Food	School	Travel

Under each heading, list as many things made of paper as you can.

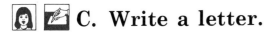 ## C. Write a letter.

1 Imagine that as part of a project your class has just visited a paper mill. Write a short letter of thanks to the manager, Mr George Sinclair. Set out your letter like the one here. Finish with **Yours sincerely** and put your own name in the next line.

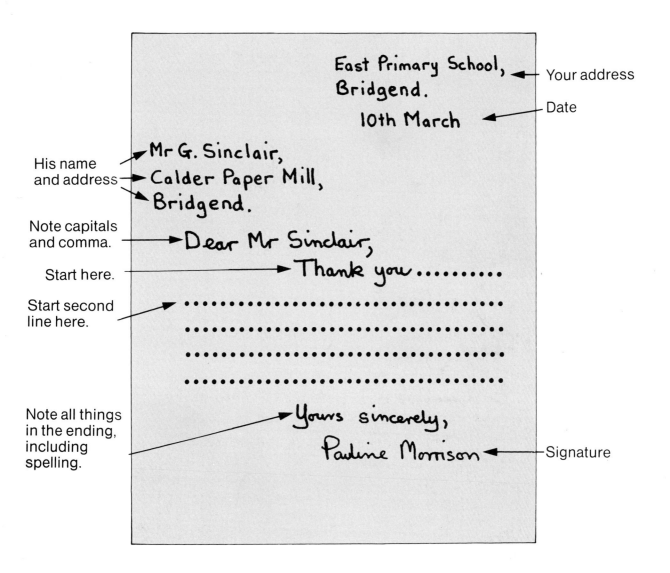

2 Draw an envelope shape.
Address an envelope to the manager.
Mark the stamp corner and show the cost of sending the letter.

D. Find out.

Look round your classroom and collect samples of as many different kinds of paper as you can find.
Now do this experiment.

Problem: to find out why we need different kinds of paper.

Discussion: (a) How do the papers differ?
 (b) What are the papers to be used for?

Activities:

1 Test each paper by (a) writing on it, (b) tearing it, (c) folding or crumpling it, (d) sprinkling water on it.
2 Note what happened to each kind of paper.
3 Write about your experiment, telling

 (a) what you did (collected, examined, talked, tested)
 (b) what happened
 (c) what you found out
 (d) why different kinds of paper are needed.

E. Spelling

hope	*hoping*
live	
move	
change	
come	
dance	
take	
write	

This unit is about paper and paper-making. The word **making** comes from the verb **to make**.
The **e** drops out before **ing** is added.
Write the list of verbs in the box, and beside each verb write the **ing** form. The first has been done for you.

 Add to your list as many more verbs ending in **e** as you can, and beside each write the **ing** form.

Exceptions: die dying   lie lying   tie tying
 dye dyeing

F. Extra

Design an anti-litter poster.

Daily Speaker

Thursday, 1st May

TRILLIONS!

World scientists probe invaders from space. Friend – or deadly foe?

Millions upon millions of tiny, hard, shiny objects descended on the village of Harbourtown yesterday.

In the windy, open sky there was slight darkening – a cloudy patch that glittered in the sunlight. Then there was the sand-stormy rattling hiss as the Trillions came. When it was over, there were drifts of Trillions everywhere.

A. Group discussion

If you lived in Harbourtown how would you feel about the Trillions? What would you do?

The Trillions

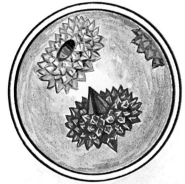

They were beautiful. It was as if he looked at priceless jewels, cut and facetted into superb circular gem-stones. Under the microscope, the colours were even more startling than they were under normal light. He increased the magnification to concentrate on one particular Trillion. It looked like a great ruby. Then he shifted the slide to what appeared as a giant emerald, with a thousand geometrical faces cut in it.

"Do you notice? Two sorts?" said Bem.

Scott looked again, comparing one Trillion with another.

"You're right, Bem. Two sorts. Only two .... One like a doughnut, with a hollow in the centre –"

"Not a hollow, a complete hole," interrupted Bem.

"And the other with –"

"The other like a doughnut again, but with a spike sticking out of the centre."

From *Trillions* by Nicholas Fisk

17

B. Writing about the Trillions

The editor of the *Harbourtown News* knows you saw the arrival of the Trillions and she has asked you to write a report for the paper. Use all the information on page 17 to help you. Write the report in your own words. Don't forget to tell:

1 what kind of day it was,
2 where you were and what you were doing when you first saw the Trillions,
3 how they arrived,
4 what they looked like,
5 how you felt and what you did,
6 whether you thought they were friend or foe,
7 what you think could be done about them.

  # C. Missing words

Write the following paragraphs, putting suitable words in the spaces. If you cannot immediately think of a suitable word, read on. You may find you can go back and fill the space quite easily. When everyone in your group has finished, compare the words that were chosen and say why some are more suitable than others.

In the dark, the Trillions formed. They came from every corner of _____ room, from the fibres of the _____, from the cracks in the floorboards. _____ meshed and geared, climbed and rolled, _____ and interlinked. Soon there was a _____ of Trillions a foot, eighteen inches _____. Still they linked and interlinked. Now _____ were climbing. They made a dark, _____ glittering patch on the blanket at _____ foot of Scott's bed. The patch _____ a wave that travelled towards Scott's _____.

Scott groaned and turned in his _____. He lay on his back. A _____ flow of Trillions fell, like sand, _____ the sheet on to his neck.

D. Speech marks

If the words in the balloons were written in story form, they would be written like this:

1 "What does it mean?" said Scott.
2 "I don't know," replied Bem.

In 1 the words from the balloon now have speech marks around them and the question mark stays in the same place. In 2 the balloon words now have speech marks around them but the full stop has been replaced by a comma.

 Note that there is a new line when there is a new speaker and that there is a full stop after Scott and Bem.

 Language marks

Full stops, commas, question marks, speech marks and exclamation marks have been left out of this passage. Write it correctly, putting in all the marks.

 Well have you ever seen anything like it before asked Scott
 I suppose there must be lots of things like it said Bem
 Mind out shouted Bem as his sister Panda came rushing in
 I bet you don't know about them she said
 Know about what asked Bem
 About the Trillion things replied Panda

Vawn

Ispex

E. Listening

On page 95 there is an extract from a book called *Sunburst* by the author of *Trillions*. Your teacher only should turn to that page and should read it to your group.

But first read this introduction which will help you to understand what the story is about. When you have heard the extract, answer the questions.

Tsu

Vawn, Tsu, Ispex and Makenzi were children left at boarding-school on Earth while their parents were building an exciting world on a new planet, Epsilon Cool. The children wanted to join their parents so they built a space ship, *Starstormer*, and blasted off into space. *Starstormer* linked with a shuttle from Epsilon Cool and they were united with their parents. Suddenly, the shuttle stopped moving. They were trapped in the world of Tyrranopolis and put to sleep. When they awoke they found themselves in a room made of blackness.

Now listen to the extract.

Makenzi

 About Sunburst

Answer in sentences.

1 What was the first change in the black room?
2 A voice gave them instructions. What did it say?
3 Why did Ispex say he wasn't going?
4 What was the second change in the surroundings?
5 Whom did the children see at the narrowest part?
6 What did the owner of the voice look like?
7 Who did the voice say he was?
8 Which of the children did not trust the laughing voice?
9 How did **you** feel as you listened to the story?

F. Planning the story

When writing stories it helps if the scenes are acted out first – even without words.

With *Space Encounter* as a title, plan a sequence which might be like this.

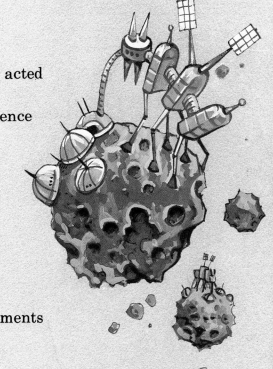

1 blast off
2 exploring the planet
3 finding rocks and plants
4 encounter with inhabitants
5 peaceful ending (or otherwise)

Act out or mime your sequence. A musical accompaniment with tuned and untuned instruments helps to stir the imagination.

G. Writing the story

A good beginning to a story makes the reader anxious to read on. This does not mean that you must always start at the beginning of events – you can begin in the middle, or even at the end.
For example:

Suddenly we came upon them! They were weird-looking creatures which struck terror into our hearts.

You can then go back to the beginning and tell the story of how you came face to face with them.

Follow this pattern and write a story called *Space Encounter*.

Remember to write in sentences, to put in all necessary punctuation marks, to take care with spelling and to read over your finished work.

"Serve them right if I drown!"

It was warm enough to swim, but too rough for Alice to use her inflatable duck. "As long as you're careful and stay close to the shore," Carrie said, when Jo asked if *she* might.

"I'll be careful, I promise," she said.

She realised she was moving fast through the water without any effort. She reared her head and saw that the tail of the duck had risen up in the wind and was acting like a sail, blowing her. She shifted her grasp towards the duck's middle but this only made its tail lift up higher. The wind was as strong as a wall and she could do nothing against it. She put her feet down but she was out of her depth and there was nothing beneath her. She thought of sharks, down in those murky depths, cruel mouths smiling, and drew her legs up.

Too scared to try and swim in case the sharks saw her legs moving, she let go the duck with one arm and waved frantically. Someone must see her! She could see *them*! Any second now, they would start shouting and screaming and rush to her rescue.

But they all went peacefully on with what they were doing. No one looked seaward, so there was no point in waving. She thought bitterly – "Serve them right if I drown!" – and for perhaps thirty seconds, drowned was what she wanted to be, to teach them a lesson. Drowned, she would be no more trouble to anyone. They would deal out her things, books for Charlie, good clothes set aside for Alice when she was older, and then forget she ever existed. They would be happy without her! She gasped, and the salt sea rushed into her mouth and down her throat, choking her. She went under the water, fought her way up, coughing and spluttering – and knew she didn't want to drown after all. She yelled into the wind, "Help me, please help ..." and, like a miracle, a voice answered her.

From *Rebel on a Rock* by Nina Bawden

A. Group discussion

"Serve them right if I drown!" – and for perhaps
thirty seconds drowned was what she wanted to be,
to teach them a lesson.

Have you ever felt you wanted to teach someone a
lesson of this sort?
What are the real reasons behind a wish like this?

 # B. About the story

1 What was causing Jo to move so fast in the water?
2 When she found she was out of her depth why didn't
  Jo swim?
3 How did Jo signal she was in distress?
4 Why did no one see her signal?
5 At first Jo wished she would drown. Why was this?
6 What made her change her mind?
7 Who was older, Alice or Jo? Give reasons.
8 Write a few sentences telling what you think might
  have happened when Jo's cries were heard.
9 There is one simile in this story. Write it.

C. Exclamation Mark (!)

Exclamation marks are used to show fear, surprise,
danger or any other excitement.
You may use an exclamation mark after a single word
– "Help!", "Oh!" or at the end of a sentence –
"Someone must see her!" "Serve them right if I drown!"

D. More about speech marks

The balloon words are the exact words spoken. If these words had been written as part of a story they might have been written like this:

"Keep shouting," called the voice, "so that I don't lose you."

called the voice has interrupted the exact words.

Look carefully at the punctuation and note that

(a) There are two sets of speech marks – one set before the interruption, and one set after it.
(b) There is a comma after **shouting** and it is written before the speech marks.
(c) There is a comma after **voice**
(d) There is a small letter at **so** because it does not begin a new sentence and it is not a proper noun.
(e) There is a full stop after **you** and it is written before the final speech marks.

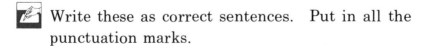 Write these as correct sentences. Put in all the punctuation marks.

1 At least said Jo I've saved the duck
2 Help me she called I'm drowning
3 The others she thought are too busy to notice
4 I hope this said Carrie will teach you a lesson
5 No one cares Jo said if I am dead or alive
6 It would have been better thought Jo if I'd drowned

E. Using punctuation marks

To **punctuate** means to **divide up**

Punctuation marks – full stop, comma, question mark, exclamation mark, speech marks – help the reader to make sense of written language.

Write these sentences, putting in missing punctuation.

1 Can you hear me

2 Save me

3 Her books her clothes her belongings would be given to the others

4 Help I'm drowning

5 I really don't want to drown said Jo

6 Keep shouting called a voice

7 Over here came the reply

8 Come quickly she called or I'll drown

Did you notice when the writer meant **said** but used another word? Look out for other examples and use them in your stories.

F. Syllables

A syllable is a sound that makes a word or part of a word. Each syllable has a vowel sound. Say these words.

Jo   shark   help   (one vowel sound)

contact   moving   seaward   (two vowel sounds)

limited   peacefully   (three vowel sounds)

inflatable   conversation   (four vowel sounds)

Make four headings in your workbook.

One syllable	Two syllables	Three syllables	Four syllables

Write the following words under the correct heading.

murky	duck	bitterly	spluttering
teach	existed	lesson	exclamation
cruel	anyone	throat	miracle

Write your name under the correct heading.
Write the names of some of your friends too.

G. Story outline

Before you write a story, short notes are helpful because:

1 you will have thought the story through to the end,
2 you will have the events in the right order,
3 you will not leave out important information.

Here is part of a story outline. Complete the outline information, then write the whole story. Take care with spelling and punctuation; write neatly, then other people will enjoy reading what you have written.

> Warm sunny day
> sandy beach
> family spending the afternoon there
> boy goes out alone in rowing boat
> one oar accidentally slips into the sea
> ebbing tide takes boat out to sea

Remember to make an exciting beginning. This does not always have to be the starting point of events.

  H. Spelling

Study these words. Write them in your workbook and add as many more to each form as you can.

thoughtful   thoughtfully   horizontal   horizontally
careful   carefully   continual   continually

Discuss the words you have written with others in your group. Say what the rule is.

"We beg, we pray ..."

Oh, books, what books they used to know,
Those children living long ago!
So please, oh please, we beg, we pray,
Go throw your TV set away,
And in its place you can install
A lovely bookshelf on the wall.
Then fill the shelves with lots of books,
Ignoring all the dirty looks,
The screams and yells, the bites and kicks,
And children hitting you with sticks –
Fear not, because we promise you
That, in about a week or two
Of having nothing else to do,
They'll now begin to feel the need
Of having something good to read.

From *Charlie and the Chocolate Factory*
by Roald Dahl

A. Discussion

Your teacher will decide whether you have class or
group discussion. The pattern for discussion is always
the same.

1 The teacher or a group leader should lead the
  discussion.
2 A time limit should be fixed.
3 Each person in the group should have a chance to speak.
4 The group leader should report on the discussion.

Topic for discussion

A television series is better than an exciting book.

Think of books you know that have also been
on television.

B. Order form

Here is an order form for books from a school book club.
Examine it, then answer the questions on page 29.
Remember to scan.

To help you complete this form, remember:

1 Minimum order, 15 books.
2 Claim **2 Free Books** for every 10 books ordered.
3 Cheques or postal orders – not cash – should be sent.
4 When complete return to

Red Circle Book Club,
New Road,
Reading.

Tally Column	Titles	Bk No.	Quantity						
			40p	45p	50p	55p	60p	£2	FREE
3	Ghastly Ghosties	60			3				
	Oil from the North Sea	61							
2	Crossword Puzzles	62					2		
5	The Magic Ruby	63		5					
2	Making Puppets	64			2				
4	Mystery at Ferryden	65		4					
3	Quick Quiz	66		3					
6	Space Encounter	67	6						
4	Goals Galore!	68			4				
4	Hidden Treasure	69					4		
3	Escape!	70		3					
1	How to Play Chess	71		1					
2	Steam Engines	72			2				
	Feathered Friends	73							
1	Fight for Water	74			1				
1	Stamp Collecting	75			1				
3	Quicksands	76					3		
1	Junior Dictionary	77						1	
Totals			A	B	C	D	E	F	FREE
			6	16	13		9	1	

C. About the form

1 What is the least number of books a school may buy?
2 How should payment be made?
3 How many books has this school ordered?
4 Which book is most popular?
5 Write the title of the dearest book.
6 Which books had no buyers?
7 What price of book had most buyers?
8 Write the full words for Bk. No.
9 What does **Tally Column** mean?
10 How many free books would be given?
11 Which free books would **you** choose?

D. Writing

Choose four of the titles. Imagine what the books would be about. Write a paragraph for each title, telling a little about the book – but not giving too much away. Write your paragraphs so that people would want to read the books.
Example:

Goals Galore!

If you are fond of football this is the book for you. Greenside Rovers were bottom of the League – until Puggy Polson joined them. Then things started to happen.

For readers of ten and over.

GOALS GALORE

GOALS GALORE

E. Library

Ten-year-old James Harrison is determined to lay the ghost that disturbs the peace of their cottage, so he and his friend Simon visit the local library to look for information about ghosts.

Ledsham Public Library, once the village prison, was a dour, solid little building in the centre of the church square. The high barred windows and sternly functional appearance were a reminder of its original purpose: inside, however, it was brighter and more welcoming, with whitewashed walls and row upon row of shelves stacked with books.

The librarian, Mrs Branscombe, sat, when she had time to sit, behind a small table laden with card-index boxes. She had been knitting the same jersey for five years, Simon claimed, presumably because most of her time was spent jumping up and down to help the short-sighted, the young and the confused. She said she was sure there must be something on ghosts. She began to hunt along the fiction shelves.

"Not fiction," said James. "Not this one anyway." Simon looked embarrassed but Mrs Branscombe had not heard.

She found two books of *Collected Ghost Stories* and offered them hopefully. The boys looked at each other.

"Actually," said James, "what we were thinking of was something kind of scientific – a sort of Guide to Ghosts."

Adapted from *The Ghost of Thomas Kempe*
by Penelope Lively

When you visit the library you will find the librarians very willing to help. Helping is part of their job.

It is a good thing, however, to know how the books are arranged.

If you are looking for a storybook (fiction) you will find that the books are arranged on the shelves in the alphabetical order of authors' surnames.

Arrange, in alphabetical order, the surnames of these authors.

Clive King   Penelope Lively   Elizabeth Beresford
Mary Norton   Roald Dahl   Astrid Lindgren
Nicholas Fisk   C.S. Lewis   Nina Bawden

If you are looking for information (non-fiction) you will find that most but not all libraries classify their non-fiction into subjects arranged by number according to the Dewey Decimal System.

Here are the 10 main classes:

> 000 General works (general knowledge, general encyclopaedias)
> 100 Philosophy
> 200 Religion
> 300 Social Sciences (education, folklore, law)
> 400 Language
> 500 Pure science (chemistry, mathematics)
> 600 Applied science (How to ...)
> 700 The Arts (painting, sculpture, music)
> 800 Literature
> 900 Geography and History

F. Find out.

Under which Dewey number would you look for information on these subjects?

(a) punctuation   (e) cookery
(b) Bible stories   (f) poetry
(c) drawing and painting (g) weather
(d) schools   (h) maps

G. Questions

Make up six questions you would ask about the extract from *The Ghost of Thomas Kempe* on page 30.

UNIT 7

Mountain Rescue

 ## A. Writing the story

These eight pictures tell a story.
They are shown in the order in which things happened.
This is called **sequence**.

Use the pictures to help you to write the story for your local paper.

Remember

Adjectives, adverbs and good choice of verbs make your story interesting. Avoid beginning sentences with <u>Then</u>. Be as careful as you can with spelling, punctuation and handwriting.

B. Commentary

Take it in turn to give a commentary on the hill walk. Each person in the group could do one section. When you wrote the newspaper story the action had already happened – it was in the past. When you give a commentary, you do so while the action is taking place. It is in the present time. You might begin this way:

Pupils from Muiredge Primary School are gathering here on this beautiful Saturday morning to climb Castle Hill. Three members of staff are with them.

. . .

The Mountain Code for Scotland

BEFORE YOU GO

Learn the use of map and compass.
Know the weather signs and local forecast.
Plan within your capabilities.
Know simple first aid and the symptoms of
  exposure.
Know the mountain distress signals.
Know the country code.

WHEN YOU GO

Never go alone.
Leave written word of your route and report
  your return.
Take windproofs, woollens and survival bag
Take map and compass, torch and food.
Wear climbing boots.
Keep alert all day.
Avoid disturbance to farming, forestry and
  field sports.

IF THERE IS SNOW ON THE HILLS

Always have an ice axe for each person.
Carry a climbing rope and know the correct
  use of rope and ice axe.
Learn to recognise dangerous snow slopes.

WHY NOT

Go on a course–

The Scottish Sports Council
1 St. Colme Street
Edinburgh EH3 6AA

Join a Club–

The Mountaineering Council of Scotland
59 Morningside Park
Edinburgh
EH10 5EZ

 C. About the code

1 Why should you never go to the hills alone?
2 Why should you plan your route before leaving?
3 What is first aid?
4 What is the meaning of: "Plan within your capabilities"?
5 Would it be advisable to take a short sleep if you felt tired?
   (Give a reason.)
6 What advantage would there be in joining a club?
7 If there is snow on the hills, why should each person
   have an ice axe?
8 Where would you find out about mountain distress signals?

D. Speech marks

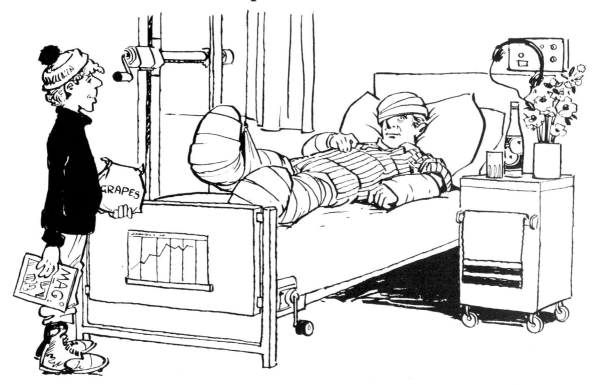

 1 In pairs act out the scene in the picture. Change roles so that you have a chance to be both patient and visitor.

 2 Write a short conversation for the picture.

Remember!

(a) Take a new line each time there is a new speaker.

(b) Put speech marks round the exact words spoken.

(c) If the speech is interrupted by *he said* or *the boy said* or *said his friend* there will be **two** sets of speech marks.

E. Design a card.

Design a get-fit-quick card for the injured climber and make up a message to write inside.

F. Pie Chart

A pie chart shows at a glance how one amount compares with another. Here is a pie chart, a circle, which is divided into twenty-four equal parts. Each of these parts represents one hour, but notice that one part (or segment) has been halved. The colour code is shown below.

A puppy's day

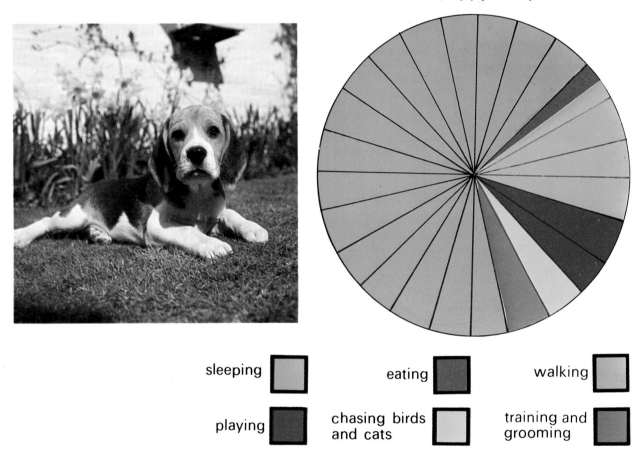

sleeping ☐   eating ☐   walking ☐

playing ☐   chasing birds and cats ☐   training and grooming ☐

About the pie chart

1 What took up most of the time?
2 How long was spent walking?
3 On which two things was an equal amount of time spent?
4 How long was spent on eating?
5 How many hours were spent playing?

Make a pie chart showing how **your** day is divided (twenty-four hours).

Checkpoint 1

1 Write the vowels in alphabetical order.

2 Write the consonant that follows each vowel.

3 Write the names of the second, fourth, eighth and twelfth months of the year.

4 Put these pictures in the right order so that they tell a story. Answer by writing the numbers only.

5 Write one or two sentences which tell how you think the story ended.

6 Add **-ed** and **-ing** correctly to these verbs.
   halt chop sob pick trap step

7 Write the following paragraph putting **to**, **two** or **too** correctly in each space.

They walked slowly in silence for a minute or _____ till they came _____ a spot which was neither _____ near nor _____ far from the deserted cottage. Sid went _____ but kept at a safe distance behind the other _____.

8 Copy this form into your workbook and complete it.

Surname _____
(capitals, please)

Forename(s) _____

Address _____

_____ Post code _____

Date of birth _____

Tel. No. (if any) _____

9 Add **-ing** correctly to these verbs.

take   come   write   dine   sing   name

10 Copy the table into your workbook. Say each word silently to yourself, then write it under the correct heading.

One syllable	Two syllables	Three syllables	Four syllables

went   interrupted   overgrown   hearing
upset   thought   insistent   respectfully

11 Write the ten different adjectives in this paragraph.

It was a golden afternoon. The hedgerows lay in neat black lines among bleached fields of stubble, and sunshine came through them in spurts. Long black fingers of shade streamed away from the elms on the hill-top and the whole wide arc of the horizon was fringed with graceful shapes of trees against the pale sky.

12 Write these sentences, putting in capital letters and punctuation.

(a) carol will be ten on saturday
(b) how old are you
(c) i will be eleven in june
(d) You will need cardboard scissors paste and paint to make the model.

13 Write these sentences putting in **there, their,** or **they're** correctly.

(a) They went to stay with _____ aunt.
(b) _____ was no bread left in the shop.
(c) If they don't come soon _____ going to miss the start of the show.

14 Complete these similes. Make them as interesting
as you can.

to scream like _____   as dangerous as _____
to talk like _____   as sad as _____

15 Write these shortened words in full.

I'll	they'll	I'm
don't	it's	he's
can't	we've	you'll

16 All the verbs in the box mean **cut**, but each has its
own special use. Write a sentence for each verb to
show that you understand its special use.

chopped	cut by striking with an axe or knife
gashed	made a long deep cut
sliced	cut into thin strips
slit	split by making a long clean cut
felled	cut down and brought to the ground

17 Write the following sentences, putting in speech
marks correctly.

What was that? whispered Anne.
I'm not sure, said Alan.
Do you think we should turn back? asked Anne.
Perhaps it would be safer, replied Alan.

18 How do you scan for information?

19 Make a flow chart for a game you play.

UNIT 9

Over His Dead Body

The Adamsons lived in one of the terrace-houses bordering the Common – old Mrs Adamson and her two sons. Ken, the elder, had always been jealous of his brother, crippled in an accident. He thought his mother spoiled his brother and neglected *him*. By the time Mrs Adamson died, and the brothers were left alone, jealousy had turned to hatred.

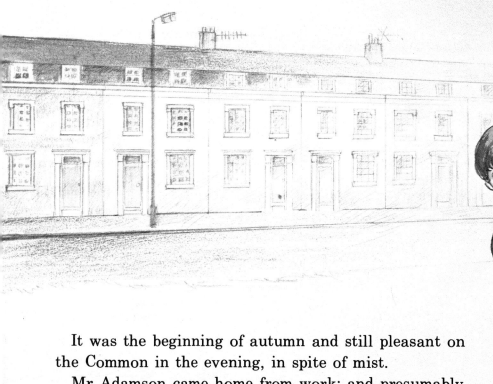

It was the beginning of autumn and still pleasant on the Common in the evening, in spite of mist.

Mr Adamson came home from work; and presumably the two brothers had supper, talked, perhaps – although Mr Adamson never spoke to his brother if he could help it – and prepared for bed. Just before bedtime, as usual, Mr Adamson must have changed into his running shorts and top and training shoes and set off on his evening run.

Questioned afterwards, the neighbours said that the evening seemed no different from any other evening. But how were they to know? The Adamsons lived in a house whose party-walls let little noise through. Would they have heard a scream? The sound of a heavy body falling – falling – ?

Some time that evening Mr Adamson's brother fell downstairs, fatally, from the top of the stairs to the bottom. Whether he fell by his own mischance (but no, in all his life, he had never had an accident on those stairs), or whether he was pushed – nothing was ever officially admitted. But the evidence examined afterwards at least pointed to his already lying there at the foot of the stairs, huddled, still, when Mr Adamson went out for his evening run. Mr Adamson must have had to step over his dead body as he came downstairs, in his running gear, to go out on the Common.

It so happened that neighbours did see Mr Adamson leaving the house. He left it looking as usual – or almost as usual, they said. One neighbour remarked that Mr Adamson seemed to be smiling. He never smiled, normally. They saw no one come out of the house with him, of course. No one followed him.

From *The Shadow-Cage and Other Tales of the Supernatural*
by Philippa Pearce

A. Group discussion

1 What is jealousy?
2 Why do you think that Ken's jealousy of his brother turned to hatred? Why didn't that hatred turn to pity after his mother's death?

B. About the story

1 Why did the neighbours hear no unusual sounds from the Adamsons' house?
2 Is it likely that Ken's brother had died before Ken came home from work? (Give a reason.)
3 Write three questions which police might have asked neighbours.
4 What was unusual about Ken's expression as he left the house to go jogging?
5 Do you think Ken killed his brother? (Give reasons.)
6 How do you think the body was discovered?

C. How observant are you?

Eye-witnesses are usually asked to give a description of somebody or something they have seen. Without turning back to look, write a description of Ken Adamson in his jogging gear. Tell the colour of his clothing and shoes. Tell the colour of his hair. Say something about his age, height, build and the expression on his face.

Now check with the picture. How observant were you?

  ## D. Character study

As you read a story, you are making up your mind about the characters of the people in the story – what kind of people they are. Sometimes, as the story unfolds, you change your ideas.

What kind of person do **you** think Ken Adamson is? Do you like or dislike him? Do you feel sorry for him because of the kind of home life he has? Will he have many friends? Write a paragraph which describes his character.

When everyone in your group has finished, take it in turn to read out the paragraphs. Discuss the differences in ideas.

 ## E. Prefix

"Did he fall by **mis** chance?"

mis is a prefix, an addition at the beginning of a word. Add **mis** to each of these words and when you have done so, write what you think **mis** means.

fortune	inform	fire	place	use
led	behave	lay	spell	understand

Check with your dictionary and add to the list.

F. Pronouns

Read this paragraph, which continues the story on page 40.

"The evening strollers on the top of the Hill had been looking at the view, and one or two had begun to watch the runner on the slopes below. **He** was behaving oddly. **They** had watched **him** change course, and then double to and fro – 'like a rabbit with something after **it**,' as one watcher said."

The words **he**, **him**, **they**, **it** are **pronouns**. Pronouns take the place of nouns. Which nouns do **he**, **him**, **they**, **it**, replace in the passage?

Now read the paragraph aloud, putting in the nouns instead of the pronouns. You will then see how useful pronouns are.

He, **him** and **it** are singular pronouns.
They is a plural pronoun.

The words in the box are pronouns.

Singular	Plural
I, me	we, us
you	you
he, him	they, them
she, her	
it	

Write these sentences, using pronouns from the box to fill the spaces.

1 The neighbours said _____ hadn't heard anything unusual.
2 Ken thought his mother neglected _____ .
3 _____ did her best for Ken's crippled brother.
4 "Did _____ hear anyone scream?" asked a policeman.
5 "_____ heard nothing," said a neighbour.
6 "Tell _____," said a policeman, "where _____ were at ten o'clock."

G. Spelling

Here are ten words. Find other words that sound exactly the same, but have a different spelling.

mist	would
two	heard
know	stairs
through	see
one	course

Discuss the meanings with members of your group.

H. Find out.

Why do you think this particular symbol was chosen for the **Find out** sections in *Wordpower*?

Perhaps it has already reminded you of the fictional character, Sherlock Holmes.

Use encyclopaedias or reference books to help you to find out more about him, for example:

Who wrote about him?
What was his profession?
How did he dress?
Where did he live?
Who was his companion?

Jazz-man

Crash and
> CLANG!

Bash and
> BANG!

And up in the road the Jazz-man sprang!
The One-Man-Jazz-Band playing in the street,
Drums with his Elbows, Cymbals with his Feet,
Pipes with his Mouth, Accordion with his Hand,
Playing all the instruments to Beat the Band!

TOOT and
> Tingle

HOOT and
> Jingle!

Oh, what a Clatter! how the tunes all mingle!
Twenty Children couldn't make as much Noise *as*
The Howling Pandemonium of the One-Man-Jazz.

(Eleanor Farjeon)

A. Discussion

1 Street musicians today usually play in big cities. Have you ever seen any? What instruments were they playing? Which will be the most profitable places to play? Would you give any of your money to a street musician?

2 Did you like the poem? Say why you did or didn't. This is a poem for speaking rather than reading. Why is this? Say it as a group.

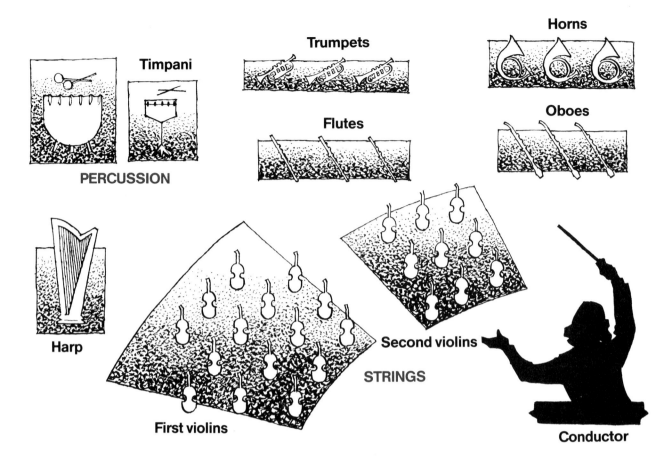

Timpani

PERCUSSION

Trumpets

Flutes

Horns

Oboes

Harp

First violins

Second violins

STRINGS

Conductor

B. The Orchestra

A symphony orchestra is divided into four families –
Strings, **Woodwind**, **Brass** and **Percussion**.
Occasionally extra instruments such as piano,
harpsichord, harp, organ, guitar or additional
percussion may be added, but these are not usually
counted as regular members of the orchestra.

Each orchestra is arranged differently either to suit
the acoustics (or sound) of the hall, or because the
conductor prefers certain instruments nearest to him.

Normally most of the strings (the most important
section) are at the front, while the noisiest instruments
(brass and percussion) are at the back. One possible
arrangement is shown in the illustration but it is by
no means the only one.

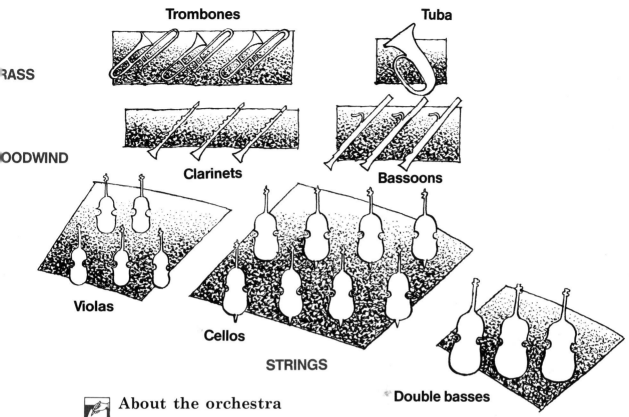

BRASS

Trombones

Tuba

WOODWIND

Clarinets

Bassoons

Violas

Cellos

STRINGS

Double basses

About the orchestra

1 Which instruments form the largest section of the orchestra?

2 Which four instruments make up the brass family?

3 Which four instruments make up the woodwind section?

4 Which section of the orchestra is the most important?

5 Name two instruments that are not regular members of the orchestra.

6 Why are brass and percussion instruments placed at the back of the orchestra?

7 If you were given the chance to learn to play one of the instruments in the orchestra, which one would you choose? Why would you choose it?

8 If you have listened to any orchestral music on radio, television, tape or record player, or if you have been to a concert hall, tell about the kind of music you enjoyed and why you enjoyed it.

Suggested listening

On record or tape: *Young Person's Guide to the Orchestra* (Britten).

C. Collective Nouns

The words in the box are **collective nouns**. That means they are singular nouns which are the names of groups of people or things. Match each collective noun with its group.

orchestra	class	army	fleet	queue
audience	team	mob	choir	flock

Group   Collective noun

1 musicians playing together   orchestra
2 soldiers
3 pupils grouped together
4 football players
5 people waiting in a line
6 ships
7 sheep
8 people singing together
9 unruly people
10 people listening

D. Plural of nouns ending in o

Musical terms that end in **o** add **s** to make the plural. Most other nouns ending in **o** add **es**

1 piano	pianos
cello	cellos
banjo	banjos
soprano	sopranos
contralto	contraltos
piccolo	piccolos
2 potato	potatoes
tomato	tomatoes

Note: Eskimo   Eskimos

Look in the dictionary for any words you don't know. Add to list 2.

✎ E. About the group

1 Make up a name for the pop group. Describe the
   appearance of the players and the instruments they
   have.
2 Describe your favourite group. Say why you like it
   and which are your favourite songs. If you have no
   favourite group, write about your favourite
   performer.

F. Find out.

Find out from information books about these
instruments. Write about each of them in your
own words and tell how each is played.

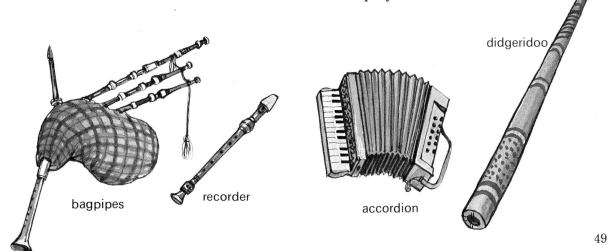

didgeridoo

bagpipes   recorder   accordion

UNIT 11

An Apple a Day

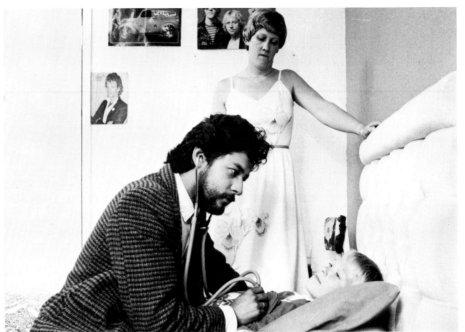

 ## A. Dialogue

Study the picture, then write a conversation that might have taken place between Tom and the doctor. Write it as it would be written in a book. Remember all the punctuation marks. Begin like this.

"Good morning, Tom," said the doctor.

"Good morning, doctor," answered Tom. "I feel awful."

Finish the conversation and try to find words to replace **said**.

B. Direct and indirect speech

The conversation you wrote between Tom and the doctor is called **direct speech**, and speech marks (or **inverted commas** as they are sometimes called) are placed round the exact words spoken. If Tom's mother tells his father about the doctor's visit, she will use **indirect speech** and no speech marks are required. His mother is reporting what happened, not repeating the exact words. Complete this indirect speech.

After you left for work this morning, Tom didn't feel well so I called the doctor. He said that ...

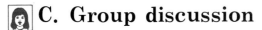

C. Group discussion

Talk about ways of keeping healthy. Think of food, fresh air, exercise, hygiene.

D. Infectious illnesses

Mumps	Measles	Chicken Pox	Whooping Cough	Scarlet Fever
	X			
	X		/	
	X	X		
X	X	X	X	
X	X	X	X	
X	X	X	X	
X	X	X	X	X
X	X	X	X	X

Here is a chart of the illnesses of the pupils in a school class. The red crosses show girls. The black crosses show boys. From a study of the chart:
(a) answer the questions and
(b) make a similar chart for your own class.

1 Which illness affected fewest children?
2 How many more cases of measles were there than mumps?
3 What was the total number of illnesses the boys had?
4 Which illnesses affected more boys than girls?
5 How many fewer cases of scarlet fever were there than chickenpox?
6 Can you tell from the chart how many people are in the class? Give reasons.

51

E. About the spray

remalgon
-for rapid relief
of muscular pain

FOR EXTERNAL USE ONLY

Directions for use

Shake well before using.
Hold the container about 15cm from the skin with
the arrow pointing to the site of the pain, and
press the button to spray in 2-3 short bursts. The
spray is rapidly absorbed by the skin.
If symptoms persist consult your doctor.

CAUTION

Pressurised container. Protect from sunlight and
do not pierce or burn, even after use. Do not spray
on a naked flame. Do not use in a confined space
or breathe vapour. Do not smoke while spraying.
Keep away from eyes.

FLAMMABLE

1 Before using the spray, or any other, what should
you do?
2 What would you use REMALGON for?
3 What are you directed to do first when using
REMALGON?
4 Write the words that tell you should not spray
REMALGON into your mouth.
5 How can you avoid spraying too big a dose?
6 The makers of REMALGON do not claim that it is
a cure. What do they claim?
7 If the pain doesn't go away after giving
REMALGON a fair trial, what should you do?
8 Write the word that tells the tin has contents that
can easily be set alight.
9 Why should REMALGON not be used in a confined
space?
10 Why is it important to have the arrow pointing
directly to the sore spot before pressing the spray
button?

F. Spelling

Doctor is a word that is often mis-spelt. Here is a
list of ten common words which, like doctor, end in **or**.

actor	motor
author	sailor
conductor	spectator
instructor	tutor
janitor	visitor

Study the words. Say them clearly to yourself,
looking at and listening to each syllable. Cover them
and write as many of them as you can remember.
Check against the list and look carefully to make
sure you have spelt them correctly. Add to your list
of **-or** words if you can.

G. Word puzzle

These are the clues to the words in the boxes. Each
answer ends in **or** and two letters of each word are
given. Write the answers in your workbook.

1 farm vehicle

2 a very great fear

3 a looking glass

4 a mistake

5 a person who betrays
  friends or country

6 a heavy piece of metal with
  hooked ends attached by a
  chain to a boat

7 a giver

8 to support or guarantee

H. Writing

Describe a time when you were ill in bed. Tell what was wrong with you, how you felt, who looked after you and what you did to pass the time.

I. Pronouns

Write the following paragraph, putting a pronoun in each space.

The doctor told Tom _____ should stay in bed and _____ left a prescription for _____ . Tom's mother took _____ to the chemist and _____ gave _____ a bottle of medicine and told _____ to give _____ to Tom three times a day.

 ## J. Prefixes

Prefixes are additions at the **beginning** of words. Write two words for each prefix on the cards. When you have done that, write down what you think each prefix means. When everyone in your group has finished, discuss the words and meanings with your teacher.

K. Extra

1 Make up a radio advertisement for a fitness campaign.
2 Make it short and snappy – they're expensive!
3 Choose a panel of judges to pick the six best.
4 Record these six on tape.
5 Listen to them as a class.
6 Vote for the one you liked best.

Jabberwocky

'Twas brillig, and the slithy toves
   Did gyre and gimble in the wabe;
All mimsy were the borogoves
   And the mome raths outgrabe.

"Beware the Jabberwock, my son!
   The jaws that bite, the claws that catch!
Beware the Jubjub bird, and shun
   The frumious Bandersnatch!"

He took his vorpal sword in hand:
   Long time the manxome foe he sought –
So rested he by the Tumtum tree,
   And stood awhile in thought.

And as in uffish thought he stood,
   The Jabberwock, with eyes of flame,
Came whiffling through the tulgey wood,
   And burbled as it came!

One, two! One, two! And through and through
   The vorpal blade went snicker-snack!
He left it dead, and with its head
   He went galumphing back.

"And hast thou slain the Jabberwock?
   Come to my arms, my beamish boy!
Oh frabjous day! Callooh! Callay!"
   He chortled in his joy.

(Lewis Carroll)

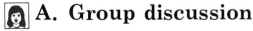 A. Group discussion

Read this poem as a group.
You won't know some of the words in it because Lewis
Carroll invented them specially. That doesn't make it
impossible to read and understand the poem. Why not?
What is the main idea of the poem?

B. Suffixes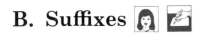

Suffixes are additions to the **end** of words.   The
suffixes on the cards were all used in *Jabberwocky*.
Under 1 are words from *Jabberwocky*.
Under 2 are other words with the same suffixes.
Write as many more words as you can with the same
suffixes.

1	2	
slithy	dusty	oily
uffish	selfish	foolish
whiffling	running	puffing
burbled	gurgled	stumbled
vorpal	final	magical
frabjous	joyous	dangerous
frumious	furious	glorious

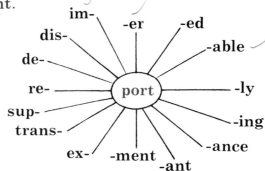

C. Root words

Root words are words in their simplest form.   By
adding suffixes, prefixes **and sometimes both**, words
can be built up or have their meaning changed.

   How many more words can you make from the root
word **port**? The diagram will help you.   Here is one:
important.

im-   -er   -ed
dis-   -able
de-   **port**   -ly
re-   -ing
sup-   -ance
trans-   -ant
ex-   -ment

duct is another root word. Use the diagram to help you to build on it. Discuss with your group and teacher the words you have made.

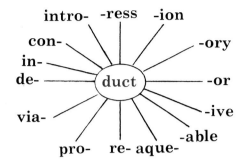

D. Sounds

Lewis Carroll, the author of *Jabberwocky*, says the Jabberwock **burbled** as it came. **Burbled** represents the sound it made. Write these phrases putting a **sound word** in the spaces. The first one is done for you.

1 The car's brakes screeched.
2 The steam _____ .
3 The drum _____ .
4 The explosion _____ .
5 The chains _____ .

E. Its, it's

Write **it's** when the meaning is *it is* or *it has*.
At all other times write **its**.
   It's time for **its** dinner.
   It's been a lovely day.
Write these sentences, putting **its** or **it's** correctly in the spaces.

1 The bicycle has lost _____ bell.
2 I think _____ safe to cross now.
3 _____ never been better.
4 If _____ raining, the game will be postponed.
5 The eagle swooped on _____ prey.

E. The Jabberwock

1 Write a description of what you think the Jabberwock looks like. Tell also about some of the things it does.
2 Make a mobile of the Jabberwock.

 # F. Spelling

More language patterns

The singular nouns in column 1 all end in **f** or **fe**. These nouns change the **f** to **v** before adding **es** to form the plural. Write the first column in your workbook and opposite each write the plural. The first one is done for you.

1	2
half	halves
calf	
thief	
leaf	
wolf	
wife	
shelf	
leaf	

Exceptions: These words add **s** to the singular.

  roof   chief   belief

Add to columns 1 and 2 if you can.

G. Extra

Make up nonsense words to fit the spaces in what might be a seventh verse of the poem. Remember that the words should follow the patterns of the English language and fit the rhythm of the poem.

I've slain the _____ Jabberwock,
  No more the _____ pest will bite;
No more its _____ claws will catch
  The _____ man who flees in fright.

Checkpoint 2

1 Write this sentence, putting in the missing commas.

The shopper took a trolley and collected milk eggs rolls cheese and bacon.

2 Write these sentences, putting **to**, **too**, or **two** correctly in the spaces.

(a) I woke _____ find it had been snowing overnight.

(b) There were only _____ prizes and I received one of them.

(c) It's _____ far _____ go on foot.

(d) He asked if he could come _____ .

3 Write these sentences putting **its** or **it's** correctly in the spaces.

(a) _____ time for bed.

(b) The river burst _____ banks.

(c) I cannot understand why _____ not ready.

4 Speech marks are missing from this conversation. Write the conversation putting in the speech marks.

Good afternoon, Polly, said the wolf. Where are you going, may I ask?

Certainly, said Polly. I'm going to see my grandmother.

I thought so, said the wolf, looking very much pleased. I've been reading about a little girl who went to visit her grandmother and it's a very good story.

Little Red Riding Hood? suggested Polly.

That's it, cried the wolf.

From *Little Polly Riding Hood*
by Catherine Storr

59

5 Read the following paragraph and then write one sentence giving the main idea.

    For weeks the older boys and girls had been trundling their guys in old perambulators and wooden handcarts round the village and even into Rye, wheedling money for fireworks. "Penny for the guy. Two pennies. Five pence," and now all the children were seething with excitement, except Kizzy.

From *The Diddakoi*
by Rumer Godden

6 Make these verbs end in **ing**.
   come try leave die look stop take

7 Write the plural of these nouns.
   car box piano potato donkey pony

8 Copy the table into your workbook and put these words under the correct headings.

One syllable	Two syllables	Three syllables	Four syllables

   rewarding yourself popular hate everlasting

9 Make a flow chart showing each stage of cleaning your teeth.

10 Write six words of two or more syllables which end in **or**.

11 Write the sentences, putting a conjunction from the box in each space.

  (a) She knitted a scarf _____ she was watching TV.
  (b) Come at six o'clock _____ you can.
  (c) _____ it's your birthday you can stay up later.
  (d) I cannot come _____ I am too busy.
  (e) Santosh is tall _____ Morag is taller.
  (f) The storm lasted into the night _____ we were kept awake.

as
because
but
while
so
if

60

12 Make two columns in your workbook. Head them
Fiction and **Non-Fiction**. Write the titles of these
books under the correct heading.

13 Here is an outline story. Write the story as a
reporter might write it for a newspaper. Finish the
story in any way you wish.

man parks car at pavement's edge – goes to buy a
newspaper – car starts to move off as lady with
pram steps on to crossing –.

14 Here are five prefixes and five words. Each
prefix goes with one of the words and makes it
opposite in meaning. Write the five new words.

un   fortune
im   well
mis   perfect
de   connect
dis   control

15 **fer** is a root word. Use the diagram to help you to build as many words as you can. Here is an example: **conference.** Check the words in a dictionary.

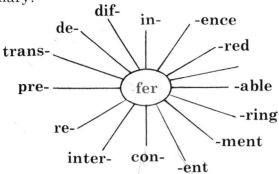

16 Write the following paragraph putting suitable **pronouns** in the spaces.

John went fishing with a friend, but _____ did not catch any fish himself. _____ both said _____ had enjoyed the outing, but when _____ went home, John's mother said _____ had been hoping to cook fish for tea.

17 Scan the poster to find this information.

(a) How much does a child pay?
(b) Where is the concert?
(c) When is the concert?
(d) Who will benefit from the concert?
(e) Who supplies the tickets?

Laughter Lines

Two men were arguing about friends of theirs. Each one thought his friend was more stupid than anyone else in the world but neither of them could prove it.

It was arranged, therefore, that they would bring their friends along, set each an impossible task and note the results.

"Hello, Tom!" said the first of them to his friend. "Here's twenty pence. I want you to go into town and get me a colour television set."

"I'll do that right away," said Tom and off he went.

"Dick," said the other, "run round to my house and see if I'm in, will you?"

"I will sir," said Dick and he was off.

He found Tom round the corner.

"Do you know, Tom," he said, "I think that's the stupidest man I've ever met. He has asked me daft things before but this beats the lot."

"I don't know about that," said Tom. "Look at this. He gives me twenty pence, tells me to get a colour television and doesn't tell me what colour he wants."

"Ah-ha," says Dick. "That's nothing. That one says to me 'Take a run round to my house and see if I'm in!' Now there's a telephone lying beside him. He could have phoned up, found out for himself and saved me all this bother."

Read the questions on page 64, re-read the story, then answer the questions.

A. About the story

1 What were the names of the two stupid people?
2 Did **they** think they were stupid? (Give a reason.)
3 How was their stupidity to be tested?
4 If you were given 20p and told to buy a colour television what would **you** do?
5 Why do you think Tom and Dick set off to carry out requests they believed to be silly?
6 Who do you think was the most stupid person in the story?
7 What are your feelings about using Tom and Dick in this way to satisfy an argument?

B. Group discussion

Did you find the story funny?
What sorts of things make you laugh?
What things, intended to be funny, do not amuse you?

 ## C. Why are they laughing?

1 Write one or two sentences about each picture to tell what you think is making each person laugh.

(b)

(a)

(c)

2 Read these three stories, then write one or two sentences to say which one amused you most and why it did. If none of them amused you, can you say why?

(a) The phone rang about 2 a.m. and the absent-minded professor answered it. "Hello", he said.

Voice: Is that Leicester twenty-one twenty-one?

Professor: No, this is Leicester two one two one.

Voice: Oh – I *am* sorry to have bothered you.

Professor: It's quite all right, I had to get up to answer the phone anyway.

(b) An excited young man ran madly down the ferry landing, leaped across two metres of water and landed with a crash on the deck of the ferry.

"Well," he gasped, as he picked himself up, "I made it!"

"What's your hurry?" asked a deck-hand. "This boat's coming in."

(c) A man called unexpectedly on a friend and was amazed to find him playing chess with his dog. The man watched silently for a minute or two and then said,

"That's the smartest dog I've ever seen in my life."

"Oh, he's not so smart," came the answer, "I've beaten him three games out of four."

D. Comparison of adjectives

This picture shows the strongest men in the world.

Jiro — strong

John — stronger

Jim — strongest

Jiro is **strong**.

John is **stronger** than Jiro.   (compares two)

Jim is **strongest** of the three.   (comparing more than two)

Copy this table into your workbook.
Complete the table.

high quick old late soon tall light	higher	highest

E. Adjectives ending in -y

1 y changes to i before adding **-er** or **-est** unless y
   follows a vowel (for example, gay, gayer, gayest).
   This class is noisy.
   The class next door is noisier
   The class in Room 7 is the noisiest of all.

Complete this table.

sunny	sunnier	sunniest
tidy		
lovely		
happy		
busy		
heavy		
pretty		
lucky		

2 Comparing adjectives of **more than one syllable,**
   other than those ending in **-y**.
   Instead of adding **-er** and **-est**, use **more** and **most**,
   like this:
   beautiful, more beautiful, most beautiful.

Complete this table.

stupid	more stupid	most stupid
comfortable		
important		
considerate		
thoughtful		
frightened		

Learn these exceptions.

much	more	most
good	better	best
little	less	least
bad	worse	worst

F. Extra

Make a class book of jokes and funny stories.

UNIT 15

Reasons for Writing

2 Green Street,
Stopley.
4th March.

Dear Ken,
It was great to hear from you.
Alfie Wilson has taken your place in the
football team and although we lost 2-1 in
Saturday's match, he had some really good
saves.
Mrs Semple has been off ill so
we've had "You·know·who" for the last
week - bet you're glad you missed that!
Any chance of spending a Saturday
in Stopley soon?
From
Mike

Shopping

Milk
Bread
Biscuits
Tomato Soup
Eggs
Sausages
Crisps
Toothpaste

Selina
Sees a Ghost

A Play in Three Acts

Surname ....
First name...............................
Address ....
....
....
....
Age ....
Date of birth...........................
Place of birth ....
Name of school ....
Class...

A. Group discussion

Throughout your writing exercises in *Wordpower* you have
been able to practise or study all the kinds of writing
shown on pages 68 and 69.

Discuss 1 the reason for writing each one, and
2 what is special about the way each one is set down.

68

B. Importance of punctuation in writing

When you speak to someone you don't have to worry about full stops, question marks, commas, exclamation marks or speech marks; your voice gives the meaning. If you don't put in punctuation marks when you are writing, the reader will find it difficult to understand. There is no punctuation in the following description.

1 Read it and try to understand it.
2 Read it again, noting the stopping places.
3 Write it correctly.

Carrie listened it wasnt the sound she had heard before but something quite different it was a queer throaty chuckling gobbling sound that seemed to come from somewhere above them higher up the path they stood still as stone the sound was coming closer
Run Carrie said
She ran and Nick ran behind her and the creature followed them.

Adapted from *Carrie's War*
by Nina Bawden

C. Spelling – common mistakes

Many people find these words difficult to spell.

length   safety   colour
beautiful   sincerely   separate

For each word do the following things.

1 Look at the word and **say** it (to yourself).
2 **Check** that you have said it correctly.
3 **Cover** the word.
4 **Write** it.
5 **Check** that you have written it correctly.
6 If you haven't, do so.

D. Apostrophe for possession

1 Look at these pictures and at what is written below each.

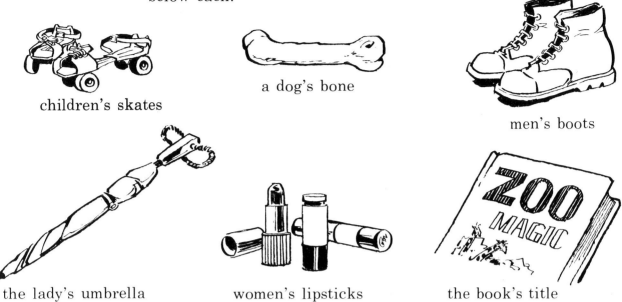

children's skates

a dog's bone

men's boots

the lady's umbrella

women's lipsticks

the book's title

There is an owner noun for each picture – children, dog, men, lady, women, book. None of the owner nouns ends in **s** so apostrophe and **s** (**'s**) are added before writing the noun that is owned.

Now look at these pictures.

ladies' handbags

cats' tails

boxes' lids

The owner-nouns above all end in **s**, so only apostrophe (**'**) is added before writing the noun that is owned.

71

2 Write these sentences putting **apostrophe and s** or **apostrophe only** in the correct places.

    (a) The boys jacket was torn.
    (b) They were invited to the childrens party.
    (c) The girls collected more than a weeks pocket money.
    (d) Tuesdays meeting was well attended.
    (e) The ladies golf match was postponed.
    (f) The boys football team won the cup.
    (g) Lisa was taken to the babies ward in the hospital.
    (h) The knives blades were very sharp.

E. Write a description.

 Look at the picture of the athlete.

Write a description of her. Remember to write in sentences. When you have written a few sentences, read them over to yourself to see how they sound. This will help you to decide what you should write next.

Remember – take care with **punctuation and spelling** and write neatly. This makes reading much more enjoyable. If you cannot write neatly first time, make a rough draft on a piece of paper, then copy it neatly into your workbook. Sometimes you find you can make improvements as you re-write.

Carnival!

This is a picture of the Notting Hill Carnival – a feast of colour with people dancing and singing in the streets to the rhythmical Caribbean music of steel bands.

Caribbean English is slightly different from standard English but some of the words from the Caribbean have come into use in standard English. Here are five of them. Look them up in a dictionary and write their meaning.

barbecue   buccaneer   calypso   hammock   hurricane

A. Dialect

Here is a Caribbean calypso called "Linstead Market." Sing it as a class and accompany it with bongos and maracas, using this rhythm throughout and also as an introduction and link between verses.

Practise the rhythm first, and to help you get it correct, say these words to yourself as you play it.

maracas

bongos

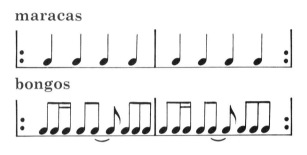

Linstead Market

Calypso   *West Indian*

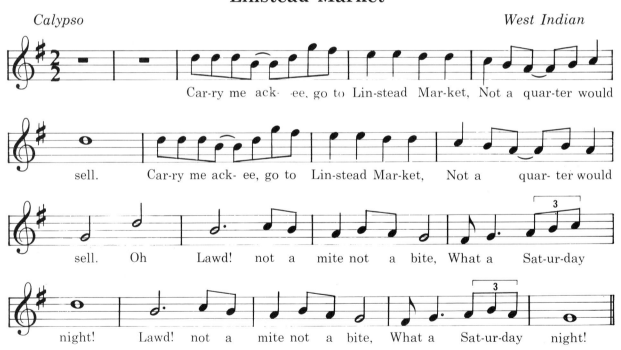

Car-ry me ack- ee, go to Lin-stead Mar-ket, Not a quar-ter would sell. Car-ry me ack- ee, go to Lin-stead Mar-ket, Not a quar- ter would sell. Oh Lawd! not a mite not a bite, What a Sat-ur-day night! Lawd! not a mite not a bite, What a Sat-ur-day night!

Verse 2

Everybody come fill up, fill up,
Not a quarter would sell.
Everybody come fill up, fill up,
Not a quarter would sell.
   Chorus: Oh Lawd! etc.

Verse 3

Make me call it louder, Ackee! Ackee!
Red and pretty they am.
Lady buy your Sunday morning breakfast,
Rice and ackee am gran'.
   Chorus: Oh Lawd! etc.

A dictionary gives this meaning of dialect:
"A way of speaking used in a particular part of a
country or by a particular group of people."

Caribbean children learn standard English in schools
and hear it on radio and TV, yet many of them talk in
dialect amongst themselves; for example, they may say:
"De sun am shinin' in de sky."

Dialect is used in the calypso, "Linstead Market."

Carry <u>me</u> ackee,   Rice and ackee <u>am gran</u>',
Red and pretty they <u>am</u>   Oh Lawd!

Although you learn to read and speak standard
English in school, perhaps you, too, have a dialect you
speak out of school. Discuss dialects you know and
give examples.

B. Write a calypso.

Work in small groups to make up a calypso to fit the
tune of "Linstead Market." You may write about
anything at all. It could be something you want to
groan about or something happy to sing about.

If you need help to get started, here are two
examples. You may use one as a first verse and add
further verses of your own.

Example 1

Going to school on a Monday morning,
Grouse and grumble and groan,
Going to school on a Monday morning,
Grouse and grumble and groan,

Chorus: Oh Lord! what a bore, what a bore –
    Same old work as before,
    Oh Lord! what a bore, what a bore –
    Same old work as before.

Example 2

Going to school on a Monday morning,
Meeting up with my pals,
Going to school on a Monday morning,
Meeting up with my pals,

Chorus: Oh Lord! what a lot we've to say –
    Chatter, chatter all day!
    Oh Lord! what a lot we've to say –
    Chatter, chatter all day!

C. Find out.

Here is a map of the Caribbean islands. Four of them have been numbered. Find out from an atlas the names of these islands.

D. Verbs

The past tense.

> He <u>called</u> out to attract buyers.
> Although they <u>heard</u>, they <u>passed</u> by.
> No one <u>wanted</u> his ackee.

The underlined verbs in these three sentences are in the past tense. The action is not happening at this very moment. It has already happened.

1 The past tense of many verbs ends in **-d** or **-ed**. Write this list of verbs in your workbook and opposite each write its past tense. Add **-d** or **-ed**. Add to your list.

Verb	Past tense
hope	
close	
bake	
arrive	
love	

Verb	Past tense
look	
pass	
crush	
dust	
paint	

2 Some verbs change their vowel sounds to form the past tense. Make a wall list of verbs which change their vowel sound in the past tense.
Keep adding to it.

Verb	Past tense
begin	began
fall	fell
write	wrote
come	came
see	saw

3 Some verbs keep the same form for the past tense.

cut   shut   cast   put   hurt   hit   beat

4 Write the correct form of past tense of these verbs:

run   say   swim   leave   think
blow   set   keep   fly
cry   eat   take   obey

76

E. Prepositions

> He took his ackee **to** the market **on** Saturday hoping **for** a quick sale but people walked **around** the stalls and did not buy **from** him.

The red words in the box are prepositions. They show a link between things or people.
The word **to** shows a link between **ackee** and **the market**.

Say what the other prepositions link.

1 The words in the circle may be used as prepositions. Write these sentences, choosing the best preposition for the space.

near on
across
under from

   (a) He wrote his name and address _____ the form.
   (b) The house _____ the road is unoccupied.
   (c) She hid _____ the bedclothes.
   (d) They had a letter _____ their son.
   (e) There is a laundrette _____ our house.

2 Make up five sentences with at least one different preposition in each.

F. Fiesta!

Ask your teacher if some time could be set aside to enjoy a session of Caribbean song, dance, poetry and story. You would, of course, have to prepare for this. A book called *Mango Spice* (published by A & C Black) contains over forty Caribbean songs. Records of Caribbean music would provide rhythm for dance. A story written in dialect can be found in *Jamaica Child* by Errol O'Connor. Your library may also be able to provide material, and art work would add interest to the session.

UNIT 17

Gymnastics

All sports have two kinds of followers – those who watch (spectators) and those who take part (participants).

Gymnastics is one sport which has increased in popularity mainly because of the amount of time given to it on television.

Those who train as gymnasts must know and observe certain basic safety rules.

(a) The apparatus in the gym must be so arranged that landings from the vault don't interfere with landings from other equipment.

(b) Equipment should always be checked before use.

(c) Mats must be placed sensibly round apparatus so that gymnasts don't land on the edge of a mat or the forming of two mats.

(d) Supervision is necessary **at all times**, and gymnasts should not attempt new exercises or exercises they are unsure of while the teacher is busy elsewhere in the gym.

(e) Gymnasts should not be left alone in the gym.

(f) A first aid kit, regularly checked, should be readily accessible.

A. Discussion

Six safety rules for gymnasts are given. Study them and give a reason for each one. Ask yourself "What would happen if . . . ?"

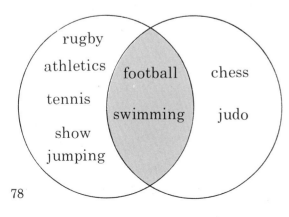

B. Venn diagram

Study the Venn diagram. In the left circle are sports or games one person likes to **watch**. In the right circle are sports or games he likes to **take part in**. The shaded area, as you can see, belongs to both circles. Make a Venn diagram of games you lik

C. Find out.

The Olympic Games are held every four years in a different place round the world. Nowadays the Games are televised and we can watch: athletics, gymnastics, swimming, horse-riding, fighting arts (wrestling, boxing, judo) and lots of other sports.

1 Choose one of the sports and find as much information about it as you can. Remember to write the information in your own words. Display and discuss what you have found out.

2 Make a list of other sports in the Olympic Games.

 # D. Abbreviations

The word **gymnastics** is often shortened to **gym**, **physical training** to **P.T.** and **physical education** to **P.E.** How would you shorten these words?

British Amateur Gymnastics Association   photograph
British Broadcasting Corporation   telephone
Automobile Association   omnibus
Her Royal Highness   perambulator

E. Awards scheme

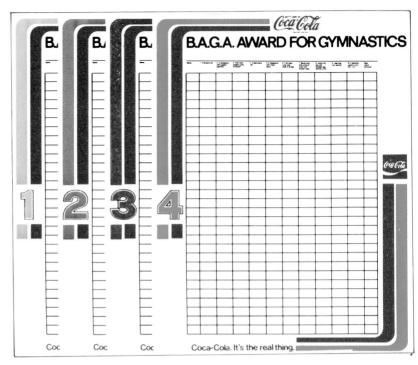

Aim of the scheme

Gymnastics is on nearly every school curriculum for both boys and girls and many of our best young gymnasts started on their way to perfection through working for the Awards. The aim of this Awards Scheme is to encourage the natural ability that all children (and adults) possess to some degree, so improving the general standard of gymnastics at local, county and national levels.

How the scheme operates

The scheme covers four sets of ten exercises, graded from the simplest level – Award 4, suitable for most children so that all can take part, to a more advanced level, Award 1, that should be within the ability range of those who have developed an interest and skill in the sport.

Entrants must start with Award 4 and work through to Award 1 to ensure the correct progression as approved by the National Technical Committees. A Personal Achievement Card for the next stage will be sent free of charge with each award.

Standard for Qualification

The standard required for the award of a badge and certificate at each level will have been achieved when any six of the ten exercises have been completed to the satisfaction of the examiner. The candidate then becomes entitled to the award badge and certificate.

Standards for performance of the exercises are entirely at the discretion of the P.E. teacher. It is stressed that our aim is to encourage children to take part in this activity and develop their aptitude accordingly.

From *Awards for Gymnastics* (British Amateur
Gymnastics Association)

 About the Awards

1 Write the heading under which you would look to find the following facts.
   (a) How well you should perform to gain an award.
   (b) At which level you should start.
   (c) What is the purpose of the scheme.
2 Which is the most difficult level?
3 How many exercises are to be performed at each level?
4 If the performer does well, what awards will be given?
5 What will be sent along with these awards?

F.

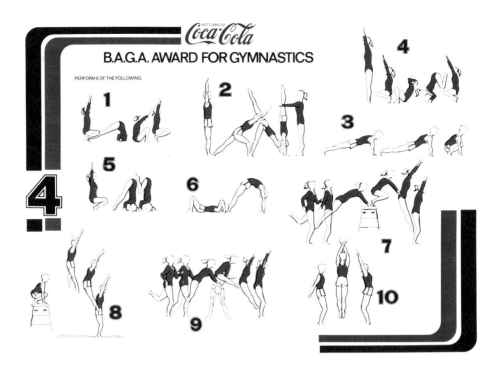

Study the chart. Opposite are descriptions of each exercise but they are not in the correct order. Start with number 1, find the description which matches the exercise and write it opposite the number. Continue in this way to number 10.

leapfrog over partner

a forward roll

a standing upward jump with turn

a headstand with knees bent

jump from box with straddle legs
  (astride jump)

from front support jump to crouch

handstand with support (partner)

a backward roll

from back lying raise body to bridge

squat onto and jump off a box with
  straight body

G. Questions

You are given the chance to interview your favourite sportsperson. Say who it is and make up seven questions you would like to ask him or her. Try to make up questions that do not have one-word answers.

H. Extra

Write a radio or TV report describing a sporting event such as the Cup Final or a Wimbledon tennis final.

The Collapso

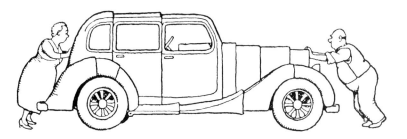

To the motorist who has no garage of his own, the "Collapso" telescopic body should prove a boon indeed. This, as the illustration shows, is so cunningly contrived that a slight push at the radiator causes every part of the car (except, of course, the extreme rear) to disappear into the part immediately behind it, somewhat to the surprise of anybody who happens to be watching.

When completely folded, the "Collapso" looks less like an automobile than one would believe possible, and can be wheeled about by hand, sent up and down in lifts, and housed for the night in the oddest places, such as cycle-sheds and wardrobes.

If this type of body has a fault (which we are unwilling to admit), it is that when involved in a collision it is inclined to fold itself unasked, with painful consequences to its inmates; but that is a small price to pay for its many unique advantages.

From *How to be a Motorist* by W. Heath Robinson and K. R. G. Browne

 ## A. About the Collapso

1 Who is the Collapso designed for?
2 How does it work?
3 What advantages are claimed for it? Are they advantages?
4 Are there any disadvantages?
5 Advertisers nowadays have to be truthful about their product. Is this advertiser truthful? Give reasons.
6 Would you buy a Collapso? Give reasons.

B. Road signs

1 Heath Robinson had his own ideas about road signs.
Match his pictures with the warnings in the box.

SCHOOL	ROUNDABOUT	SLOW
BEND	NO ENTRY	HIDDEN TURNING

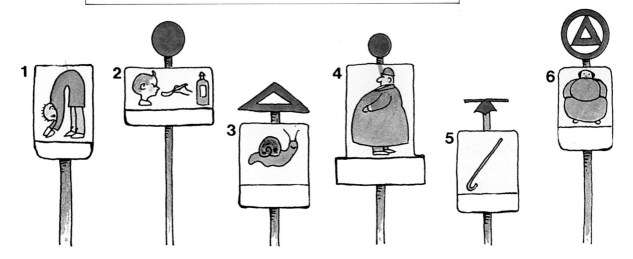

2 Make some crazy road signs of your own for these warnings.

C. Buying a bike

1 Here are some advertisements for secondhand bikes
and a telephone conversation between a seller and
someone who wants to buy a bike. Study them, then
go on to 2.

Buyer: Hello, is the Raleigh 14 still for sale?

Seller: Yes.

Buyer: Are you first owner?

Seller: No. I bought it secondhand.

Buyer: What are the tyres like?

Seller: Fairly good.

Buyer: What about the paintwork?

Seller: I've repainted it. It looks like new.

Buyer: Are there lights?

Seller: Lights and reflector, all in good order.
Would you like to come and see it?

Buyer: Where do you live?

Seller: 5 Greenfield Court.

Buyer: Where's that?

Seller: Do you know the bus station?

Buyer: Yes.

Seller: OK – first left after the bus station as you go
towards the football ground.

Buyer: I know where you are. When do you want
me to come?

Seller: 7.30 tonight?

Buyer: Fine. See you then, goodbye.

Seller: 'Bye.

2 Choose another of the advertised bikes and write a
telephone conversation like the one above. Ask for
information about brakes, saddle, handlebars, pedals
and extras (accessories). Note that speech marks are
not used when a conversation is written in this form.

RALEIGH Children's bikes at reduced prices at **ROBIN WILLIAMSON CYCLES. Tel. 225 3286.**

CITY CYCLES (EDIN.), 87 Slateford Road. Tel. 337 2351. Raleigh, Kalkhoff, Puch, Gitane, Claude Butler, Dawes. Accessories, parts, repairs. Barclay, Access, Credit.

GENT'S 19 in. bike, excellent condition, 3 speed, kickstand, carrier, £55 o.n.o. Tel. 225 2978 after 4 p.m.

TANDEM. Pashley, five-speed, excellent condition, carriers and lights included £180. Phone 554 2155 after 5.30 p.m.

RALEIGH 14 Bicycle, suit 6-12 years, good condition, saddle-bag, stabilisers £35. 332 1669.

NEW AND OLD BICYCLES bought for cash. Tel. 669 6316.

FOLD-UP bicycle, foreign, super de-luxe model, good condition, £29. Tel. 669 4887.

FOLDING bicycle, as new, 3-speed, several accessories. Tel. 332 8375 evenings.

GENTS 25″ Rudi Aitig, 10-speed, good condition, £70, plus extras. Tel. 339 3684 after 5 p.m.

RALEIGH Rodeo, suit 8-10 year old boy, £18 o.n.o. Tel. 557 2509.

CARLTON lightweight racer, chrome frame, five speeds, alloy wheels, £49.50 o.n.o. Tel. 447 4242

PEUGEOT Lady's Bicycle, 21″ frame, 10 gears, carrier, dynamo, good condition, £80. Tel. 336 1910 after 6 p.m.

D. Prepositions

Write the following paragraph, putting the correct preposition from the box in each space. Some prepositions may be used more than once.

I was interested _____ the bicycle so I went to see it. I asked _____ the tyres and commented _____ the fact that there was no bell. I quite liked the bike but I was a bit disappointed _____ its condition and didn't want to part _____ so much money _____ it. The seller disagreed _____ me _____ the price, but finally agreed _____ a reduction.

about	in
for	with
to	on

E. Cycling safely

Read all the information below, then use it to list things cyclists should and should not do. Use these two headings.

Do	Don't

Make sure your bike is safe to ride. At night you must have front and rear lamps and a rear reflector. Your brakes, lamps and reflector must be kept in proper working order. Make sure your tyres are in good condition and are properly pumped up. It is a good idea to fit a bell to your cycle and to use it, if necessary, to warn other people on the road that you are coming.

When you are riding, you should
(a) always keep both hands on the handlebars unless you are signalling,
(b) always keep both feet on the pedals,
(c) never hold on to another vehicle or another cyclist,
(d) never carry a passenger unless your cycle has been built to carry one,
(e) never ride close behind another vehicle,

(f) never carry anything unless in a saddle-bag,

(g) wear light-coloured or reflective clothing,

(h) never lead an animal.

F. Find out.

1 The bicycle in the picture below is called a Penny Farthing. Find out what you can about this bicycle.

2 Here are three other early machines. Choose one of them, find out about it and design an advertisement that might have persuaded people to buy it.

(a) hobbyhorse

(b) Kirkpatrick bicycle

(c) boneshaker

G. Writing

You have been asked to choose a new bicycle as a birthday present. What kind of bike would you choose? Write brief notes about the handlebars, gears, brakes and lighting and about any extra equipment you would save up for. Make some drawings to illustrate your descriptions.
Spelling note: Can you spell **bicycle** correctly?

H. between, among

among for more than two
between for two only

I had difficulty in choosing one bicycle from **among** so many. Finally I had to choose **between** two.

Write these sentences, putting **among** or **between** correctly in the spaces.

1 Fiona divided the apple _____ Helen and Keith.
2 The three boys managed to find enough money _____ them to buy the comic.
3 Jack and his wife finished the meal _____ them.

I. Pedal power

How safe would **you** be as a cyclist?
There is one correct answer to the questions in the
four sections below. Write the correct answer in
Sections 1 and 2. Write a description of the correct
sign in Section 3 and the correct signal in Section 4.

Section 1 As you are riding towards traffic lights, the
amber light is showing. Which colour
shows next?
(a) amber with green
(b) amber with red
(c) red
(d) green

Section 2 You may ride on only one of these. Which
one?
(a) the pavement
(b) a pedestrian precinct
(c) a motorway
(d) the street

Section 3 Which of these signs means no cycling?

    (a)   (b)   (c)   (d)

Section 4 You are riding at a safe distance behind a
car. The driver gives a hand signal to show
he is slowing down. Which is it?

    (a)   (b)   (c)

Checkpoint 3

1 Only one of the following is a sentence. Write the sentence.

(a) Because we stood still.
(b) In the dim light they saw the shape of a figure on the roof.
(c) While we clambered over the wall shouting to the others to follow.

2 Write these headings and under each write three **nouns**.
fruit   months   metals   surnames

3 Write these sentences. Put **to, too** or **two** correctly in the spaces.
He retreated _____ his bedroom _____ try _____ finish his book. It was much _____ exciting _____ stop now. Perhaps the other _____ wouldn't notice he had gone.

4 Give these words **ed** and **ing** endings.
look   try   skate   travel   dance   turn
play   carry   shriek   wait

5 Write these words in their short form, using apostrophe for missing letters.
it is   we are   can not   do not
I am   they are   could not   you have

6 Write the **main idea** of this paragraph.

Just beyond the hedge a small tree was growing. In the branches of the tree, looking very unsuitable – for he was about half its size – but very pleased with himself, was the Armitage's enormously large black cat, Walrus, so called because he wore his top front teeth outside his chin. The teeth were sticking out now even more than usual as he dangled self-consciously over two branches of the tiny tree.

From *The Looking-Glass Tree* by Joan Aiken

90

7 Put **capital letters** and **punctuation marks** in these sentences. Write the sentences.

   (a) is there another book by the same author
   (b) help i've caught my foot in some netting
   (c) flour butter sugar and eggs are required to make the cake

8 Write the days of the week in order. Begin with **Sunday**

9 Write these sentences, putting **its** or **it's** correctly in the spaces.

   (a) The dragon guarded – treasure.
   (b) – too good to be true.
   (c) The dog wagged – tail excitedly.

10 Arrange these words in alphabetical order.

   anemone marigold carnation tulip crocus daffodil chrysanthemum

11 Choose one of these book titles. Imagine what it is about and write a paragraph which would tempt others to read it.

12 Write the plurals of these singular nouns.

   town   glass   box   leaf   lady   knife donkey piano potato child   woman tooth

13 Write these words under the correct heading.

under   confirm   refill   magnify   beautiful
aeroplane   introduce   instantly   information
ability   competition

One syllable	Two syllables	Three syllables	Four syllables

14 Write the following paragraph putting suitable
words in the spaces.
It was a wooden barn with an open doorway like
the one at the turkey farm, but with a loft on
top.   There was straw on the floor, _____ a few
household throw-outs like bottomless _____ and old
toys.   You got up _____ the loft by a ladder
but _____ had shoved it up there.   You _____ only
see the edge sticking out _____ the trapdoor.   A
man with a _____ stick could probably hook the
ladder _____ easily enough.   We didn't have a
walking stick.

From *Run for Your Life* by David Line

15 Here are five **prefixes** and five
words.   Match each prefix with a
word to make the word opposite in
meaning.

mis-   arm
de-   spell
in-   healthy
dis-   control
un-   accurate

16 (a) Write four words with the same ending as care**ful**.
   (b) Write four words which have **i** before **e** when
       the vowel sound rhymes with **ee**.
   (c) Write four words with the same ending as truth**fully**.
   (d) Write four words with the same ending as continu**ally**.

17 In the following sentences, some words should have an apostrophe to show ownership. Write the sentences, putting apostrophes in the correct places.

(a) Look for the book in the childrens section.
(b) Georges brother is fourteen.
(c) They didn't finish the mornings work.
(d) You can buy ladies handbags in the shop across the road.

18 Write these sentences putting **there**, **their** or **they're** correctly in the spaces.

(a) They forgot to take _____ wellingtons.
(b) Are _____ any seats for the concert?
(c) _____ not expected until tomorrow.

19 Speech marks and punctuation are missing from this conversation. Write the conversation with the correct speech marks and punctuation.

My mother heard me going downstairs an hour early
She called out Where are you going
    Out for a bit I won't be long I said
    What about your breakfast she asked
    I'll have it later I called back
    You can't go out without it she said but I *was* out then

From *Run for Your Life* by David Line

20 Make a flow chart to show how you would replace an old torch battery with a new one.

21 Make as many words as you can with the root word **form** and the **prefixes** and **suffixes** given.

per-		-ed
in-		-ation
trans-	form	-ing
re-		-er
con-		-al
de-		-ally

Extra

Design the bicycle of the future.

Listening extracts

These are the extracts for pages 10 and 20. They can be read directly or taped for future use.

The House of Sixty Fathers

The sampan drifted along on the swollen river, carrying Tien Pao and his little pig helplessly towards the war-torn village from which his family had just escaped. Tien Pao wondered if the soldiers would still be there, and if they were, what would happen to him.

When Tien Pao reached land, he hid in a cave.

Tien Pao shoved his face hard against the little pig's side to stifle his sobs.

In the muffled cave behind the leaves, his face pressed against the sleeping pig, Tien Pao had to let go, had to cry himself out. And then he slept. And while he slept, night fell.

It was deep, dark night when Tien Pao awoke. He cautiously pushed away some of the leaves and peered out of the cave. The mountains lay in thick silence. Tien Pao listened long. Then to his ears came a slight sound and the blood started pounding in his ears. He clung to his pig. Something was coming in the dark, came running – running straight toward him and the cave. Tien Pao's heart stood still. Long frozen moments later he began to realise that the soft running sound was the sound of the river.

From *The House of Sixty Fathers*
by Meindert DeJong

Sunburst

The room shifted and changed its blackness. A
corridor formed. One of the lanterns left its place and
floated slowly towards the entrance to the corridor.

"Only the children," said the voice. "Follow the
lantern, if you please."

Ispex said, "I'm not going. They're *separating* us,
splitting us up. Why don't people *think*?" But eventually
he walked forward with the others, following the lantern.

Suddenly the corridor became a hall of golden glass,
which seemed to expand even as they entered it – no,
not a hall, it was rather as if they had entered a great
glass flask: they were standing in the widest part of it
and at the far end, a long way distant, the flask
tapered to a narrow, curved neck. The neck was
brighter than the place where they stood.

In the narrowest part of the neck, there was a single
figure, robed in golden whiteness and seated in what
could have been a throne.

"Closer!" said the figure's voice. "Come closer!"

The Emperor's voice was different, yet clear, silvery
and frail. "I am the Octopus Emperor," it said. "Yes,
truly I am. The *Octopus Emperor* . . . ." It began to
laugh. The laughter was so gentle, so full of
enjoyment, that Vawn smiled; and Makenzi; even
Ispex. Only Tsu's face stayed unmoved and masklike.

They approached the figure. Now they could see it
clearly: a very old man, white and silver, wrapped in a
thin, almost invisible veil of gold-tinged glassiness.
The figure beckoned them closer. They obeyed,
smiling: the figure radiated enjoyment and kindliness.

From nowhere, a brilliant bird appeared; flew to his
hand and perched on it. The bird thrust its beak into
the Emperor's curled fist. The Emperor opened his hand
a little to allow the bird to find the seeds concealed in it.
"Greedy villain!" murmured the Emperor affectionately,
stroking the bird's head. Then – "But no, *I* am the villain."

From *Sunburst* by Nicholas Fisk   95

Acknowledgments

The author and publishers are grateful to the following for granting permission to include copyright material in this book: George Allen & Unwin for an extract from *Charlie and the Chocolate Factory* by Roald Dahl; British Amateur Gymnastics Association for extracts from their Awards Scheme; Jonathan Cape Ltd for extracts from *The Looking-Glass Tree* by Joan Aiken, *Danny the Champion of the World* by Roald Dahl and *Run for Your Life* by David Line; The Countryside Commission for Scotland and the Scottish Sports Council for the *Mountain Code for Scotland*; Gerald Duckworth & Co Ltd for an extract and illustrations from *How to be a Motorist* by W. Heath Robinson and K.R.G. Browne; Faber and Faber Ltd for an extract from "Little Polly Riding Hood" in *Clever Polly and the Stupid Wolf* by Catherine Storr; Victor Gollancz Ltd for extracts from *Carrie's War* and *Rebel on a Rock* by Nina Bawden; William Heinemann Ltd for an extract from *The Ghost of Thomas Kempe* by Penelope Lively; Hodder & Stoughton Ltd for extracts from *The Trillions* and *Sunburst* by Nicholas Fisk; Lutterworth Press for an extract from *The House of Sixty Fathers* by Meindert DeJong; Macmillan Ltd for an extract from *The Diddakoi* by Rumer Godden; Oxford University Press for "The Jazz-Man" by Eleanor Farjeon; Penguin Books Ltd for an extract from "The Running-Companion" in *The Shadow-Cage and Other Tales of the Supernatural* by Philippa Pearce (Puffin Books 1978, pp. 83–4, © Philippa Pearce 1977); and Janie Struthers for the poem "Loneliness".

We are also grateful to the following for supplying photographs for reproduction: BBC Hulton Picture Library (p. 87, i); J. Allan Cash Ltd (p. 77); City Art Gallery, Manchester (p. 4 (a), (j)); Daily Telegraph Colour Library (p. 73); J.S. Library International (p. 4(b)); London Features International Ltd (p. 5 (h)); Longman Group Ltd (pp. 6, 50, 64); The Mansell Collection (p. 4 (c), (d), (g), p. 5 (i), (k)); Panther Photographic International (p. 36); Rex Features Ltd (p. 4, (e), (f)); S & G Press Agency (pp. 72, 79, ii–iv); Science Museum, London (p. 87, ii–iv—ii and iv are British Crown Copyright); Mark Shearman (p. 79, i) and John Topham Picture Library (p. 45).

Finally, the author would like to thank Ann Dean, Schools Library Adviser, Lanark Division, Strathclyde Regional Council and Alastair Hendry of Craigie College of Education, Ayr, for their advice and help in the preparation of this book.